B-2 Visitor Visa Application: Coming to the U.S. to Visit and How to Do It

ATTORNEY BRIAN D. LERNER

Law Offices of Brian D. Lerner, A Professional Corporation

Attorney Brian D. Lerner

B-2 Visitor Visa Application

B-2 Visitor Visa Application:
Coming to the U.S. to Visit and How to Do It

Written by Attorney Brian D. Lerner

Disclaimer and Terms of Use:

Effort has been made to ensure that the information in this book is accurate and complete. However, the author and the publisher do not warrant that this particular petition will mirror or be exactly as your situation. There has not been any attorney-client agreement created by the purchase of this petition or application. No legal advice has occurred. The cases, regulations and/or statutes cited may change at any time without notice.

Print ISBN: 978-1-948774-76-5
Ebook ISBN: 978-1-948774-75-8

INTRODUCTION

There are a multitude of different immigration petitions and applications. They are complex and full of requirements. Obviously it would be best to hire and immigration attorney to best prepare the petitions and application. However, this can certainly cost thousands of dollars.

The next best option is to get a sample of the petition written by an experienced immigration attorney. The samples cost a fraction what would be charged by an immigration attorney. However, while the reader has to alter, amend and change the parts of the sample petition to reflect their actual situation, it is a fantastic roadmap for them to use. If the reader has purchased the entire petition or application, they will have real live samples of cover letters, forms, declarations, affidavits and the necessary exhibits to use. The samples come from real cases and the names of those clients have been redacted to protect the privacy of that person or corporation.

These are petitions and applications that have been drafted by an experienced immigration attorney with over 25 years of experience. Get the benefits of that experience without the costs.

ABOUT THE B-2 APPLICATION

Want to visit the U.S.? Want to come to the United States to visit family, see sights, or travel around the states? The B-2 visitor visa application is what you will need. If approved, then you could get 6 months to come and visit the U.S. However, as many as you know, it will be rejected because the officer does not believe you will return home to your country. The law says your presumed to not want to return. This sample B-2 Visa is for you. It has everything necessary to give you the best chance possible to get an approval. Just input your own information and use the application as a guide. It has been prepared by an expert Immigration Attorney. Thus, this book will allow you to see a guide of how it is done, prepared and submitted.

TABLE OF CONTENTS

About the Law Offices of Brian D. Lerner

The Law Offices of Brian D. Lerner, APC. The law practice consists of Immigration and Nationality Law and everything involved with and regarding immigration which includes citizenship, investment visas, family and employment visas, removal and deportation hearings, appeals, waivers, adjustment, consulate processing and all types of immigration and citizenship matters. Thousands of families have been reunited and/or permitted to stay in the U.S. and/or return to the U.S. because of the successful work of Immigration Attorney Brian D. Lerner.

This law offices handles all types of immigration cases including family based and employment based. Immigration issues range from immigration court proceedings to trying to fix what paralegals may have done that was neither correct nor proper. Foreign nationals must have experience lawyers admitted to practice law.

The Law Offices of Brian D. Lerner, APC, handles cases arising from business visas, work permits, Green Cards, non-immigrant visas, deportation, citizenship, appeals and all areas of immigration. The Law Offices of Brian D. Lerner, APC does EB-5 Investor Visas, H-1B Specialty Occupation, L-1 Intracompany Transferee, E-2 Treaty Investor, E-1 Treaty Trader, O-1 Extraordinary Ability among others. Regarding immigrant visas for the Green Card, the firm does PERM and advanced degree PERM, Family Petitions, and Extraordinary Alien Petitions. In addition to affirmative petitions, the Law Firm represents people in deportation and removal hearings, including political asylum, withholding of removal, and convention against torture cases.

Brian D. Lerner has been certified as an expert in Immigration & Nationality Law by the California State Bar, Board of Legal Specialization sicne 2000 and has been re-certified three times. He now passes on his decades of experience by allowing the Reader, Law Schools, Professors and other Immigration Attorneys to purchase sample petitions on every facet of Immigration Law.

SECTION 1
Attorney Cover Letter

STATE BAR OF CALIFORNIA
CALIFORNIA BOARD OF LEGAL SPECIALIZATION

LAW OFFICES OF
BRIAN D. LERNER
A PROFESSIONAL CORPORATION

CERTIFIED SPECIALIST IN IMMIGRATION AND NATIONALITY LAW
ADMITTED TO THE UNITED STATES SUPREME COURT
ADMITTED TO THE U.S. COURTS OF APPEALS FOR THE 1ST THROUGH 11TH CIRCUITS

LONG BEACH, CALIFORNIA (562) 495-0554 | LOS ANGELES, CALIFORNIA (323) 454-7591 | MAKATI, PHILIPPINES (+632) 738-7008

January 30, 2015

Embassy of the United States of Amca
1075 West Pender Street
Vancouver, British Columbia
V6E 2M6
Canada

RE: Application for B2 Visitor Visa
Applicant: [New Applicant]

Dear Sir/Madam:

In support for her application for B2 Visitor Visa Application, i [New Applicant] hereby submits the following documents.

Forms:

1. G28 Notice of Appearance as Attorney

Table of Exhibits:

Exhibit No	Description
"1"	Declaration of applicant
"2"	Valid Passport
"3"	Copy of certificate of family registration and its translation
"4"	Bank Statement of Accounts
"5"	Medical Certificate
"6"	Police Certificate
"7"	Employment Certificate
"8"	Proof of Legal Status in Canada
"9"	Proof of ownership
"10"	Previous Visas
"11"	DS160 Confirmation page.

I.
Eligibility for Classification for a B2 Visitor Visa Application (Tourism/Pleasure)

The US Department of State's Foreign Administration Manual (FAM) has set guidelines for visa officials on determining whether to grant status to applicants. In 9 FAM 41: 31 N1 Temporary Visitors, the US Department of State indicated factors to vfy the entitlement to Temporary Visitor Application. Assessed by a consular officer, applicants must: a) Have a residence in a foreign country, which he do not intend to abandon b) Intend to enter the United States for a pod of specifically limited duration and c) Seek admission for the sole purpose of engaging in legit-imate activities relating to business or pleasure. Taking into account all above mentioned factors, applicant should be entitled to temporary visitor visa.

On the other hand, FAM also indicates if an applicant for a B1/B2 Visa fails to meet one or more of all the above mentioned crita, the consular officer must refuse the applicant under section 214(b) of the INA.

In determining eligibility for classification as a B2 visitor for pleasure, the significant factor is whether there is a clear intent on the part of the applicant to continue his or her foreign residence and not abandon the applicant's existing domicile and loved ones from his or her home country. As discussed infra, Applicant meets the eligibility requirements for classification as a B2 visitor for pleasure pursuant to the Act and her visitor visa application should be approved. Furthermore, [New Applicant] is not inadmissible as she never committed fraud or crime.

A: Intention to Return to a Residence in a Foreign Country

Applicant [New Applicant] has a complete and honest intention of returning to her location of residence in Canada. [New Applicant] was born in Philippines, is a **Japanese national**, and has lived in Canada. **See Exhibit 2 and Exhibit 3**. [New Applicant] and her daughter are accustomed to Canadian way of life and have no intention of eventually relocating to the United States. **See Exhibit 1**.

Furthermore, [New Applicant] has based her financial and business ties in Canada. She owns several parcels of profitable land property in Canada and maintains a residence with her children in Canada. **See Exhibit 9**. She has not demonstrated interest in the past to relinquish her property interests in Canada and nor does she presently. [New Applicant] has had successful business enterprises in Canada, and coupled with her numerous properties, makes more than enough money to support herself and her family very comfortably. **See Exhibit 4 and Exhibit 9**. [New Applicant] continues to make investments in her business in Canada and shows no intention of leaving it.

Canada is [New Applicant]'s chosen country and it is where [New Applicant] intends to continue living. [New Applicant] is happy and prosperous within her country and has no desire to obtain a B2 visa for the purpose of maintaining a permanent residence within the United States. Also, she is employed as a Guest Service Representative in Holiday Inn & Suites in Vancouver, British Columbia, Canada. [New Applicant] only seeks to obtain a temporary visitor's visa to bring her daughter to World Disney in Florida. **See Exhibit 1**. [New Applicant] seeks a specific allotted time to spend with her family members. After her allotted time to visit her daughter in the United States, [New Applicant] completely intends to return to Canada, to return to her liveli-

B: Intention to Enter the United States for Specific Limited Duration

[New Applicant]'s sole intention to enter into the United States is to bring her seven year old daughter to World Disney in Florida. **Exhibit 1**. In 9 FAM 41.31 N3.1, the United States Department of State has stated that the pod of time requested in the United States must be consistent with the purpose of the trip. The applicant must establish with reasonable certainty that departure from the United States will take place upon completion of the temporary visit (a limited pod of stay). Additionally, 9 FAM 41.31 N3.2 states that the applicant must have specific and realistic plans for the entire pod of the contemplated visit.

[New Applicant]'s plan to visit and bring her daughter to World Disney can be realistically performed with the time allowed with a B2 visa.

C: Intention to Enter the United States for the Sole Purpose to Legitimately Engage in Pleasure

In order to determine whether an applicant is entitled to Temporary Visitor Classification, a consular officer must determine whether the applicant has intent to enter the United States solely to engage in a legitimate activity for a limited duration. The Foreign Affairs Manual provides that a consular officer should determine that there is a legitimate activity relating to pleasure if there is no reason to believe that the applicant will engage in unlawful or criminal activities while in the United States as a visitor and if the applicant has adequate funds to avoid unlawful employment. 9 FAM 41.31 N4. [New Applicant] has no history of breaking any laws within her country and has no history of breaking any immigration laws. [New Applicant] maintains a clean record in her own country. **See Exhibit 6**. [New Applicant] has legitimate motives in requesting a Temporary Visitor Classification and there are no reasonable grounds to believe that she is entng the United States in order to commit a criminal or immigration violation in the future. Furthermore, [New Applicant] has no intention of entng into the United States in order to commit the crime of unlawful employment. [New Applicant] has a very rewarding career in Canada and has stable, happy and comfortable family life in Canada.

Her sole intention to enter the United States is for the purpose to legitimately engage in pleasure as she wishes to take her seven year old daughter ld Disney in Florida and intends to return after the said visit.

II. All of Applicant's Costs for the Visit Will Be Borne by the Applicant

As evidenced by Applicant's bank statements for her business in Canada, Applicant has sufficient means to cover the costs associated with the temporary visit. Also, as stated under oath in her Declaration, the Applicant wants to visit the United States to take her daughter to the 'World Disney' in Florida, U.S. [New Applicant] has sufficient funds for herself and her daughter in order to take care of her financial needs in the United States. **See Exhibit 4 and Exhibit 9**. As of beginning of the 2014 year, [New Applicant] has the amount of $426,101.12 in her bank account in Canada which converts to about $376,913.86 in U.S. Dollars. This amount is more than sufficient to sustain her financially in the United States in a short expand of time.

Therefore, the Applicant can and will pay for all costs associated with Applicant's temporary visit.

III. The Applicant is Not Coming to the United States to Provide Services or Engage in Business Activities that are Primarily for the Benefit of a U.S. Employer

The purpose of visit of the Applicant, [New Applicant] in the United States is to taker her daughter to the "World Disney" in Florida, U.S. **See Exhibit 1** [New Applicant] is not coming to the United States to provide services or engage in any kind of business activities that are for the benefit for a U.S. employer. She is employed in Canada in 'Holiday Inn &Suites' as a Guest Service

Representative and intends to carry on the same. **See Exhibit 7** The sole purpose of visit of the Applicant is pleasure. [New Applicant] has no intention whatsoever to carry on business activities or to provide services to a U.S. employer.

IV.
Additional Consideration of Good Health

The Foreign Affairs Manual has stated that aliens are ineligible for visas on health related grounds if any alien is determined to have a communicable disease of public health significance. 9 FAM 40.11 (See also INA §212(a)(1)(A)(i)). [New Applicant] does not have any communicable diseas-
es
of public health significance that would cause a consular officer to exclude her or render her ineligible for a B2 visa. **(Exhibit 5)**

V.
Additional Consideration of Promoting International Travel

The policy of the United States Government is to facilitate and promote international travel between the United States and other foreign countries. The guidelines explicitly state that the "policy of the U.S. Government is to facilitate and promote international travel and the free movement of all nationalities to the United States both for the cultural and social value to the world" (emphasis added) 9 FAM 41.31 N5. Accordingly, the consular officer should give a favorable disposition for [New Applicant] because the United States favors a policy that promotes international travel that has a valid social value. The value of [New Applicant]'s visit gives great social and family value.

VI.
Conclusion

Based on all the above, [New Applicant] can demonstrate that she is entitled to Temporary Visa Classification because she meets all the factors that are highlighted in 9 FAM 41.31 N1.

Therefore, in adherence to these guidelines, the consular officer should grant this visa in the applicant's favor. Through undersigned counsel, the Applicant respectfully submits that she has sufficiently demonstrated her qualification for the requested status. Therefore, we ask that her visitor B2 visa application be approved.

Please contact our office at (562) 4950554 if you have any questions or require additional information.

Sincerely,

Brian D. Lerner
Attorney at Law

SECTION 2

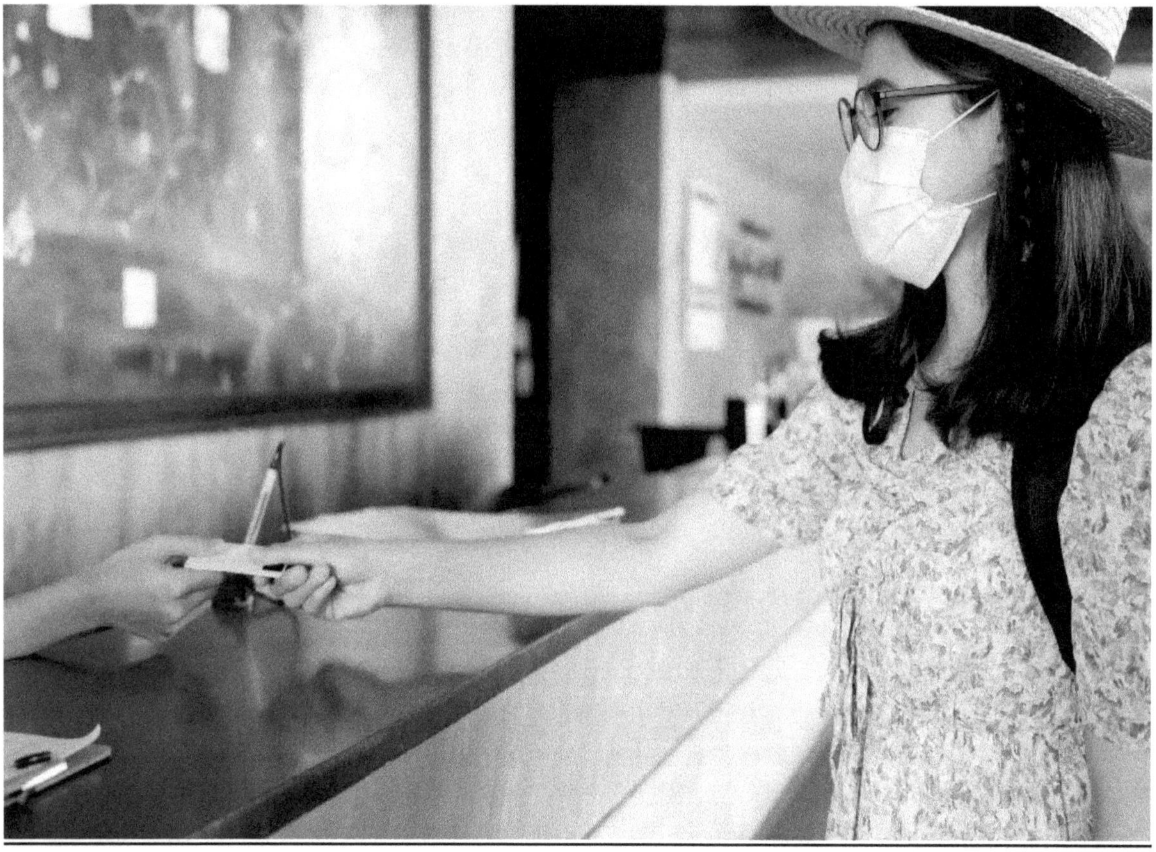

FORM G-28

DHS
Form G-28
OMB No. 1615-0105
Expires 02/29/2016

Notice of Entry of Appearance as Attorney or Accredited Representative

Department of Homeland Security

Part 1. Information About Attorney or Accredited Representative

Name and Address of Attorney or Accredited Representative

1.a. Family Name (Last Name): Lerner

1.b. Given Name (First Name): Brian

1.c. Middle Name: D

2. Name of Law Firm or Recognized Organization: Law Offices of Brian D Lerner

3. Name of Law Student or Law Graduate:

4. State Bar Number: 158536

5.a. Street Number: [illegible]

5.b. Street Name: E Broadway

5.c. Apt. ☐ Ste. ☐ Flr. ☐

5.d. City or Town: Long Beach

5.e. State: CA 5.f. Zip Code: 90803

5.g. Postal Code:

5.h. Province:

5.i. Country: U.S.A.

6. Daytime Phone Number: (562) 495-0554

7. E-Mail Address of Attorney or Accredited Representative: blerner@californiaimmigration.us

Part 2. Eligibility Information For Attorney or Accredited Representative

(Check applicable item(s) below)

1. ☒ I am an attorney eligible to practice law in, and a member in good standing of, the bar of the highest court(s) of the following State(s), possession(s), territory(ies), commonwealth(s), or the District of Columbia.

   1.a. Supreme Court of California

   1.b. I (choose one) ☐ **am not** ☐ **am** subject to any order of any court or administrative agency disbarring, suspending, enjoining, restraining, or otherwise restricting me in the practice of law. (If you are subject to any order(s), explain fully in the space below.)

   1.b.1.

2. ☐ I am an accredited representative of the following qualified nonprofit religious, charitable, social service, or similar organization established in the United States, so recognized by the Department of Justice, Board of Immigration Appeals pursuant to 8 CFR 292.2. Provide the name of the organization and the expiration date of accreditation.

   2.a. Name of Recognized Organization

   2.b. Date Accreditation expires (mm/dd/yyyy) ▶

3. ☐ I am associated with

   3.a.

   the attorney or accredited representative of record who previously filed Form G-28 in this case, and my appearance as an attorney or accredited representative is at his or her request. If you check this item, also complete **number 1 (1.a. - 1.b.1.) or number 2 (2.a. - 2.b.)** in Part 2 *(whichever is appropriate)*.

4. ☐ I am a law student or law graduate working under the direct supervision of the attorney or accredited representative of record on this form in accordance with the requirements in 8 CFR 292.1(a)(2)(iv).

Part 3. Notice of Appearance as Attorney or Accredited Representative

This appearance relates to immigration matters before (select one):

1. [X] USCIS - List the form number(s)

1.a. [illegible]

2. [ ] ICE - List the specific matter in which appearance is entered

2.a.

3. [ ] CBP - List the specific matter in which appearance is entered

3.a.

I hereby enter my appearance as attorney or accredited representative at the request of:

4. Select only one: [X] Applicant [ ] Petitioner [ ] Respondent (ICE, CBP)

Name of Applicant, Petitioner, or Respondent

5.a. Family Name (Last Name)

5.b. Given Name (First Name) [illegible]

5.c. Middle Name

5.d. Name of Company or Organization, if applicable

NOTE: Provide the mailing address of Petitioner, Applicant, or Respondent and not the address of the attorney or accredited representative, **except when a safe mailing address is permitted on an application or petition filed with Form G-28.**

6.a. Street Number and Name [illegible]

6.b. Apt [ ] Ste. [ ] Flr. [ ]

6.c. City or Town [illegible]

6.d. State 6.e. Zip Code

7. Provide A-Number and/or Receipt Number

Pursuant to the Privacy Act of 1974 and DHS policy, I hereby consent to the disclosure to the named Attorney or Accredited Representative of any record pertaining to me that appears in any system of records of USCIS, ICE, or CBP.

8.a. Signature of Applicant, Petitioner, or Respondent

8.b. Date (mm/dd/yyyy) ► 02 / 02 / 2015

Part 4. Signature of Attorney or Accredited Representative

I have read and understand the regulations and conditions contained in 8 CFR 103.2 and 292 governing appearances and representation before the Department of Homeland Security. I declare under penalty of perjury under the laws of the United States that the information I have provided on this form is true and correct.

1. Signature of Attorney or Accredited Representative

Brian D. Lerner

2. Signature of Law Student or Law Graduate

3. Date (mm/dd/yyyy) ►

Part 5. Additional Information

1.

SECTION 3
Exhibits

Valid Passport

Latest Passport of the Applicant

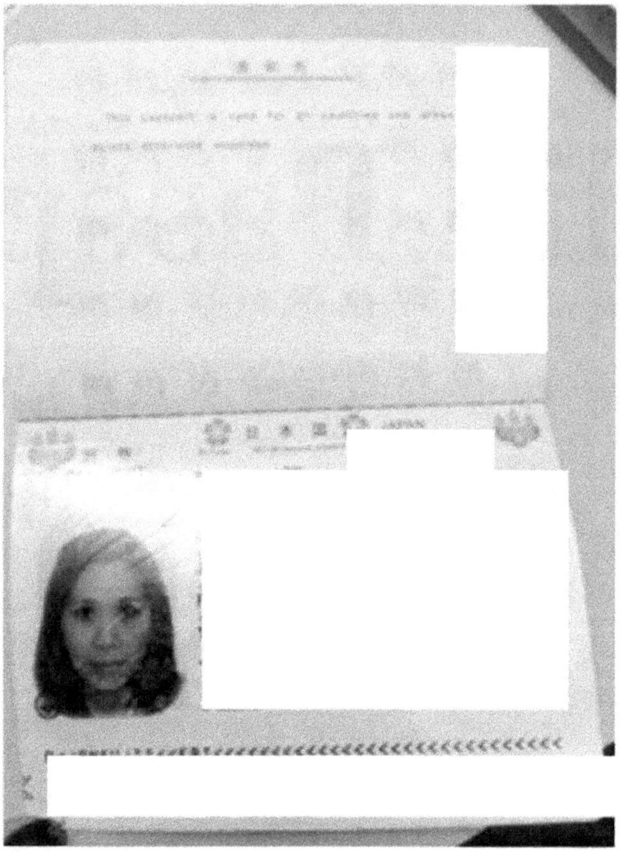

Copy of Certificate of Family Registration

'14年 7月 9日 (水) 0:47 PM FAX 番号: P. 1

1110 Howe Street
Vancouver, B.C. V6Z 1R2
t: (604) 684-2151
f: (604) 684-4736
1-800-663.9151
www.hivancouverdowntown.com

Holiday Inn & Suites
VANCOUVER DOWNTOWN

June 27, 2014

To Whom It May Concern:

Please be advised that Fujii has been employed at the Holiday Inn & Suites since April 22, 2014.

is one of Holiday Inn Hotel & Suites' valued employees, and is employed full time as a Guest Service Representative in our rooms department. current rate of pay is $16.07 per hour.

Should you have any questions with regards to the above, please do not hesitate to contact the undersigned.

Yours truly,
HOLIDAY INN & SUITES

Larry S. Ripplinger
Hotel Controller

This certificate contains security features.

Certification of All Items

Death of Spouse	Date of Death of Spouse: August 9, 2012
Person of Record in Family Register	N Date of Birth: May 6, 2007 Father: Takeshi Fujii Relationship: First daughter
Personal Item(s) Birth	Date (Place Date (Notifi Date (Notifi Notifi...
	No entry below

Issue Number: 00049060-20120814-34104003-Nishi Ward, Hiroshima City, Hiroshima Prefecture COPY [Watermark]

This document certifies all the items recorded in the family register.

August 14, 2012

Yoshio Mimura
Head of Naka Ward, Hiroshima City [SEAL]

Copy of Bank Statements

Prepared by:

Berta Arruda, CUST SERV REP
329 NORTH RD STE 400
COQUITLAM , BC , CAN V3K 3V8
Phone: (604) 933-4900
E-mail:

	Balance	Description
)0 6317894	$25,525.04	
9400 6657323	$16,312.10	
16799912	$9,054.79	
	$26,505.04	
00 7438686	$52,312.91	
·400 6286238	$14,375.18	Overdraft Limit: $300.00
IT - 9400	$282,016.06	
	USD $12,760.67	
TD Assets: CDN	$426,101.12	
TD Assets: USD	$12,760.67	
)tal Assets: CDN	**$426,101.12**	
otal Assets: USD	**$12,760.67**	

)0 ·

TR CARD -

) Liabilities: CDN

Liabilities: CDN

Prepared for:

As at: July 4, 2014

TD Assets:

Account(s)

MUTUAL FUND NON-REGISTERED
Held with TD Investment Services

MUTUAL FUND RESP - FAMILY PL
Held with TD Investment Services

MUTUAL FUND RSP - PERSONAL -
Held with TD Investment Services

MUTUAL FUND TFSA -
Held with TD Investment Services

MUTUAL FUND NON-I
Held with TD Investment Services

TD ALL-INCLUSIVE B

TD HIGH INTEREST S
6317648

BORDERLESS PLAN -

TD Liabilities

Medical Certificate

Dr. Nazila Soltani
MD

Dr. Soltani Medical Clinic
#6-2755 Lougheed Hwy, Port Coquitlam BC V3B 5Y9
Phone: 604 552 9140
Fax: 604 552 9141

MEDICAL CERTIFICATE

Re: DOB 02 Sep 1965

Certificate written: 30 Jul 2014

This is to certify that today I have examined
She is physically and mentally healthy.

Dr. N. Soltani Khorshidi
MD

30 Jul 2014 10:31 AM, Fuji, En - PHN:
[illegible]

May contain confidential info.

Police Certificate

Royal Canadian Mounted Police

Gendarmerie royale du Canada

ROYAL CANADIAN MOUNTED POLICE

Canada

Employment Certificate

1110 Howe Street
Vancouver, B.C. V6Z 1R2
t: (604) 684 2151
f: (604) 684-4736
1-800 663.9151
www.hivancouverdowntown.com

Holiday Inn
& Suites
VANCOUVER DOWNTOWN

June 27, 2014

To Whom It May Concern:

Please be advised that has been employed at the Holiday Inn & Suites since April 22, 2014.

is one of Holiday Inn Hotel & Suites' valued employees, and is employed full time as a Guest Service Representative in our rooms department. current rate of pay is $16.07 per hour.

Should you have any questions with regards to the above, please do not hesitate to contact the undersigned.

Yours truly,
HOLIDAY INN & SUITES

Larry S. Ripplinger
Hotel Controller

Proof of Legal Status in Canada

Canada

Proof of Ownership

STATE OF TITLE CERTIFICATE

300150

REMEDIOS & COMPANY
STE 1010-1030 W GEORGIA ST
VANCOUVER BC V6E 2Y3

YOUR FILE NUMBER:
8289002

LAND TITLE DISTRICT: NEW WESTMINSTER, BRITISH COLUMBIA

CERTIFICATE NO: STSR1031340 TITLE NO: CA2831934

THIS IS TO CERTIFY THAT AT 05:55 ON 22 NOVEMBER, 2012, THE STATE OF THE TITLE TO THE LAND DESCRIBED HEREIN IS AS STATED AND IS SUBJECT TO THE NOTATIONS APPEARING BELOW. THIS CERTIFICATE IS TO BE READ SUBJECT TO THE PROVISIONS OF SECTION 23(2) OF THE LAND TITLE ACT (R.S.B.C. 1996 CHAPTER 250) AND MAY BE AFFECTED BY SECTIONS 50 AND 55-58 OF THE LAND ACT (R.S.B.C. 1996 CHAPTER 245).

REGISTRAR

APPLICATION FOR REGISTRATION RECEIVED ON: 25 OCTOBER, 2012
ENTERED: 08 NOVEMBER, 2012

REGISTERED OWNER IN FEE SIMPLE:
ERI FUJII, FRONT DESK AGENT
3466 DALEBRIGHT DRIVE
BURNABY BC
V5A 3E5

TAXATION AUTHORITY:
CITY OF BURNABY

DESCRIPTION OF LAND:
PARCEL IDENTIFIER: 012-443-166
LOT 4 DISTRICT LOT 58 GROUP 1 NEW WESTMINSTER DISTRICT PLAN 79769

LEGAL NOTATIONS:
HERETO IS ANNEXED EASEMENT D56177 OVER THE NORTHERLY 5 FEET
OF LOT 210 PLAN 33825

CHARGES, LIENS AND INTERESTS:
NATURE OF CHARGE
CHARGE NUMBER DATE TIME

COVENANT
AB237245 1988-11-09 14:24
REGISTERED OWNER OF CHARGE
DISTRICT OF BURNABY
AB237245
REMARKS: INTER ALIA
L.T.A. SECTION 215
INTER ALIA

COVENANT
AB237248 1988-11-09 14:25
REGISTERED OWNER OF CHARGE
DISTRICT OF BURNABY
AB237248
REMARKS: INTER ALIA

LAND TITLE ACT

STATE OF TITLE CERTIFICATE

TITLE NO: CA2831934 PAGE: 2

Previous Visas

VISAS
IMMIGRATION OFFICER
DEPARTED
FUKUOKA A.P.
6. APR. 2005
IMMIGRATION
5019
5031
8. APR 2005
26 DE 2001
V.I.A./A.I.V.
821
HONG KONG
-6 APR 2005
8 APR 2005
27.12.03
KANSAI
21. SEP. 2007
IMMIGRATION
2120
NOV 2 3 2002
27

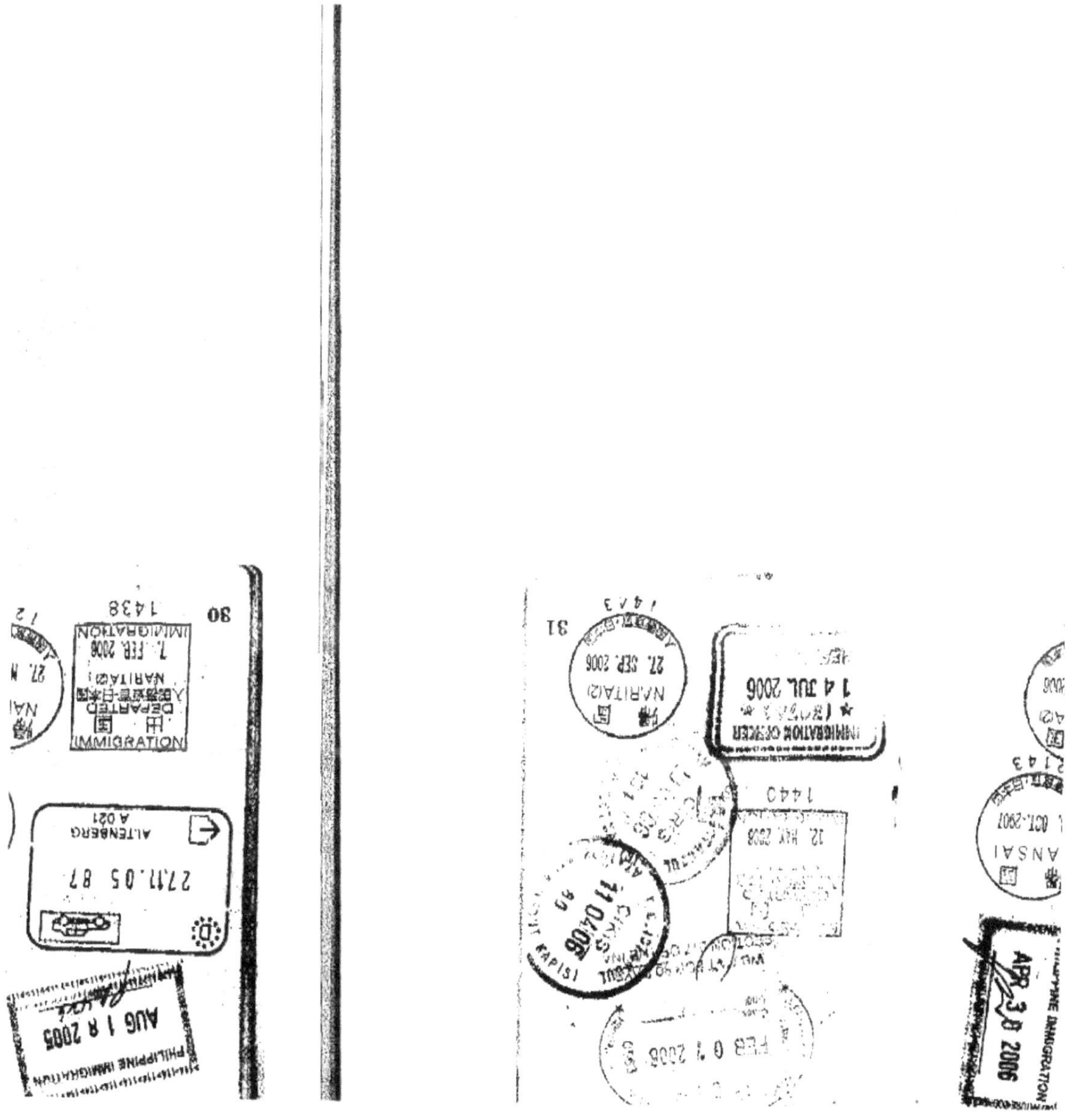

DS-160 Confirmation Page

Non-immigrant Visa Application

I: Complete Online Application (DS-160)

- Go to https://ceac.state.gov/genniv/ and select "Retrieve an Application".
- Put your Application ID: AA004A9TGU
- S ecurity Questions: Five letters surname-**[New Applicant]** Year of birth-**1965**
  In what city did you meet your spouse/significant other?- **Vancouver**

- Answ er each question.

- Uploa d photo
  - 1 inch
  - Latest photo (6 months)
  - White background
  - Full face view
  - Neutral face expression

NOTE: Please do not forget to click SAVE. DO NOT submit the form.

II: Pay fees (USD$160)

Payment options:

Online:

1. P lease log into https://usvisa-info.com/en-ca/selfservice/login

2. Follow instructions to select Trip Purpose, preferred Consulate to schedule an appointment, and other details related to your visa application.

3. NO TE: You will be asked to make a MRV fee payment or, if you have already paid the MRV fee, you will be asked to confirm your payment by entng the "MRV Fee Receipt Number"

3. The MRV fee payment can be made using the following options: • Credit Card payment: Visa, MasterCard, or Amcan Express

1. Please select the appropriate card from the provided list.

2. Follow directions to complete the transaction.

- Cash payment at one of the branches at Scotiabank:

1. Please select "Scotiabank"

2. Click on the "PDF" link next to the "MRV Fee Receipt Number" box.

3. Print the electronically generated deposit slip for each applicant.

4. Complete the relevant information.

5. Take the deposit slip(s) to the Scotiabank branch and pay the appropriate fee amount.

   - The "MRV Fee Receipt Number" is located at the bottom of the Scotiabank deposit slip in the "sal number" field. Each applicant requires a separate "sal number."

6. Return to this Web site and, when asked, enter the "MRV Fee Receipt Number" (from the "sal number" field).

- **Over the Phone:**

3. You can pay your MRV fee over the phone by Visa, MasterCard or Amcan Express using the automated voice system. Please call the appropriate number from the list below and follow instructions to make a payment.

   - Click here for telephone numbers for Canada.

4. Onc e you have paid the MRV fee and your credit card transaction has been approved, you will be provided a confirmation number. If you have family members also applying, you must repeat the payment process for each person. You must provide this confirmation number(s) in order to submit the visa application and schedule an appointment.

5. **IM PORTANT: Please write your confirmation number down immediately because you will not be able to retrieve it later.**

3. You c an speak with a call center agent to help you schedule an appointment or you can return to this website and log into your account.

4. **IMPORTANT: If you do NOT register on this Website or through the Call Center service your MRV fee cannot be associated with your name and records and you will not be able to schedule an appointment!**

Schedule an Appointment: https://usvisa-info.com/en-ca/selfservice/login

SECTION 4
Applicant Declaration

I, [New Applicant], declare the following:

I hereby certify and confirm that I am competent to give the following information based on my personal knowledge of all the facts in this declaration, unless otherwise stated, and that the following facts are true and correct to the best of my knowledge, and if called upon to testify, I would do so.

1. My name is [New Applicant], I am 49 years of age and was born on September 2, 1965 in Samar, Philippines.

2. I am a Japanese national and currently I stay in British Columbia, Canada with my family. I am employed in Holiday Inn & Suites in Vancouver, British Columbia, Canada, since April 22, 2014 as a Guest Service Representative.

3. My first overstay in the United States was in the year 2007. I got my United States visa granted on Mar 31, 2007 which was valid till June 30, 2007. But during that time, I gave birth to my second daughter, [New Applicant] in the United States and at the same time my elder daughter, who was already staying in the U.S. was sexually molested. I and my husband were in the United States to provide support for my daughter. We were there in the U.S because of the child molestation case of my eldest daughter and we were co-operating with the authorities at Fontana, California. My daughter was a victim that's why we had to stay back for support and help our daughter to get through. My daughter was undergoing post-traumatic stress because she was sexually molested. It isn't easy for parents to go through all this. It was a very difficult time for all of us and especially for my daughter. We left the United States on July 18, 2007, and therefore, we overstayed for 18 (Eighteen) days due to the reason mentioned above.

4. My second overstay was in the year 2008. The United States visa was granted on April 24, 2008 and the validity of the visa was till July 23, 2008. But I left the country on August 14, 2008. I overstayed for 21 (Twenty-one) days in the Unites States. The reason for my overstay was that my eldest daughter was diagnosed as having PTSD (Post Traumatic Stress Disorder) after she was sexually molested in the United States. She used to start shaking uncontrollably while under stress. I was there with my daughter to provide her support and help her cope through the

disaster. Also, it was the time she was graduating from her college. So I stayed back to provide support to my daughter and to make sure that she is well taken care of.

5. The reason that I wish to travel to United States is that I want to take my seven year old daughter Ms. Mai Anne Fujii to 'World Disney' in Florida.

6. We intend to come back to Canada after our visit in the Florida in the United States. Canada is our home now and we are very happy here. My family is financially well off and we own a house in Canada. My youngest daughter goes to French emersion here and also attends Junior Figure Skating Program. We have a lot of potential and opportunities that fits our lifestyle.

7. Canada fits our needs as I and my family has comfortably settled in Canada. It will always be our home and Japan will be our second home. So, there is absolutely no possibility even remote that we will move to the United States. We live a very stable, happy and comfortable lifestyle in Canada.

8. This declaration also intends to assure that I will never overstay in the United States. The reason I overstayed on two occasions was to provide support and help my elder daughter who was going through severe traumatic stress because she was sexually molested as a child in the U.S.

9. I hope that the above information describes the reason of my overstay in the United States and my intention to return back to Canada after the intended visit in Florida (U.S.) with my younger daughter.

I declare under the penalty of perjury pursuant to the Law of the State of California that the foregoing is true and correct.

I sincerely thank you for your consideration.

My Education:

Three years of business school, attending Marymount California University and Moorpark Community College.

(Focus)

-Entrepreneurship
-Management
-Economics
-Business Plan Preparation
-Business Law
-Small Business Start-up

(Special Projects in College)

Garbology Project - Investigated the garbage problem in Los Angeles and other parts of America. Visiting waste management facilities in Torrance and Santa Ana we were able to come up with solutions to solve the problem. Each member of the team sent a letter to the San Pedro government including our ideas and solutions, a lot of us including myself were sent a letter in return thanking us for our input.

Small Business Project - Three other students and myself were given a project to create a business that could be successful in this economy and plan out every detail of the business until actually paying for rent and getting a business license. We had to pitch the business to a group of teachers from the business program at Marymount California University. My group was awarded second place.

(Memberships in College)

-MCU Golf Team
-Moorpark International Student Group

(Volunteering)

-Boys and Girls club in San Pedro, California
-San Pedro Nursery

www.ingramcontent.com/pod-product-compliance
Lightning Source LLC
LaVergne TN
LVHW060045210926
848481LV00013B/3956